M000296636

A-Z

Steps to Leadership

Congratulations!
I am very proud of you and I hope
you enjoyed your school year
Make sure you keep Allah (SWT)
Prophet Mohamed (SAW)
and the Quran in your hearts
Ms. Tefour
2021/2022

Presented to ....

....

....

From ....

Date ....

A-Z

Steps to Leadership

*from the Qur'an and Words of
the Prophet Muhammad*

compiled by

Abdul Ghani Ahamed Barrie

Goodword
B·O·O·K·S

First published 1997
Reprinted 2012
© Goodword Books 2012

Goodword Books
1, Nizamuddin West Market
New Delhi-110 013
Tel. 9111-4182-7083, 4652-1511
Fax: 9111-4565-1771
email: info@goodwordbooks.com
www.goodwordbooks.com, www.goodword.net

Islamic Vision Ltd.
434 Coventry Road, Small Heath
Birmingham B10 0UG, U.K.
Tel. 121-773-0137
Fax: 121-766-8577
e-mail: info@ipci-iv.co.uk, www.islamicvision.co.uk

Non-Profit Bookstore
Talim-ul-Islam Community Center
86 Rivalda Road, Toronto ON M9M 2M8, Canada
Tel. 416-740-7844
email: lugatulquran@hotmail.com, www.LQToronto.com

IB Publisher Inc.
81 Bloomingdale Rd, Hicksville
NY 11801, USA
Tel. 516-933-1000
Fax: 516-933-1200
Toll Free: 1-888-560-3222
email: info@ibpublisher.com, www.ibpublisher.com

Printed in India

CONTENTS

Ability   9

Bravery   11

Calmness   13

Dependability   15

Exemplariness   17

Fairness   20

Genuineness   22

Honesty   24

Initiative   26

Judgement   28

Knowledge   30

Liberalism   33

Modesty   35

Nobility   37

Organization   39

Personality   42

Quality   43

Responsibility   44

Sacrifice   46

Teamwork   48

Understanding   50

Versatility   52

Wisdom   54

Youth   56

Zeal   58

INTRODUCTION

To excel in leadership, one must have very special qualities. Some acquire such qualities as they grow more mature, while others possess them from the outset. The latter are called "born leaders", the Prophet Muhammad being the best example. His conduct and qualities made it possible for him to excel in all branches of management and leadership to a degree which is still unmatched to date. Young, would-be leaders should, therefore, endeavour to acquire these exceptionally befitting qualities, so as to surpass all others in the field of management, thus achieving the goal of leadership.

A successful leader is one who attains his ends in the best possible manner, with the least inconvenience to the team, at the minimum cost, in record time and with a high-quality performance. With modern techniques, there are several ways of doing this, but the path adopted by the Prophet Muhammad (ﷺ) is the best, for it was with the divine guidance of Allah that he became the supreme leader of the human race. "Truly, in the Messenger of Allah, you have an excellent example." (The Qur'an, 33:21)

Present-day leaders could parallel at least a part of his achievement, if they did their utmost, not for selfish ends, but for the sake of Allah, and if they anticipated their rewards only from Him.

For easy reference, the characteristics necessary for leadership are listed below in alphabetical order. Supporting extracts from the traditions of the Prophet Muhammad (ﷺ) and the applicable, translated verses from the Qur'an appear in the pages that follow.

ABILITY

Let there become of you a nation
that shall call for righteousness,
enjoin justice and forbid evil.
Such men will surely
triumph.

(The Qur'an, 3:104)

In one tradition it is mentioned
that towards the end of
the world, people will occupy
positions for which they
are not suited.

(Hadith)

An Ansari from Medina once requested the Holy Prophet: "Why do you not appoint me as an executive as you have appointed so and so?" He replied, "You will see discrimination after I am gone, but be patient till you meet me on the banks of the Kausar (Fountain in Paradise)."

(Hadith of Bukhari)

Indeed people are like camels, out of a hundred you will hardly find a single one fit to ride

(Hadith of Bukhari)

The leader must be capable of performing his duties. This is a basic requirement, as success depends on an able performance. One should never take up a position without first being certain of being able to meet its demands, and one should not appoint anyone to a post for which he is not suitable. This is possible only if one is true to oneself and *brave* enough to face the facts. In essence, this means enjoining good and forbidding evil.

BRAVERY

Muhammad is the messenger of Allah and those who follow him are firm and unyielding towards the unbelievers but merciful towards one another.

(The Qur'an, 48:29)

The strong believer is better and more beloved of Allah than the weak one, although there is good in both of them. But you should never say if this is done or that is done. Do your best and leave the rest to Allah.

(Hadith narrated by Abu Hurayra)

"After me there will be discrimination and you will observe things of which you will disapprove." A companion asked, *"Messenger of Allah, what do you command us to do in such a situation?"* He replied, *"Discharge your duties and supplicate Allah for His bounties."*

(Hadith of Bukhari and Muslim)

"Whenever the fight grew fierce and the eyes of the fighters were red, we used to resort to the Prophet for succour. He was always closest to the enemy."

(Hadith of Bukhari)

The leader or manager has to be brave and strong. He should never fear the consequences of his decisions. He should simply do his best and leave the results in the hands of Allah. The really able leader should be bold, yet *calm* when deciding on matters of importance.

CALMNESS

*It is He who sent down tranquillity
into the hearts of the believers
that their faith might
grow stronger.*

(The Qur'an, 48:4)

*You who believe, be patient,
discipline yourselves and
hold yourselves together.
Heed God so that you
may prosper.*

(The Qur'an, 3:200)

*Being calm and behaving in a
manner worthy of respect is as
good as the making of sacrifices.*

*Indeed Allah is gentle and loves
gentleness, and gives an
approval
to gentleness which He does not
give to harshness.*

*The strong man is not the
one who overcomes others
by his strength, but the one
who, though angry, controls
himself.*

(Hadith of Bukhari)

Calmness is an essential quality for a leader. He
should be patient, gentle and of stable mind in
order to take the right decisions. He will thus
display his *dependability*.

DEPENDABILITY

Those who faithfully observe their trusts and their promises...are the heirs of Paradise; they shall abide in it forever

(The Qur'an, 23:8)

You who believe, stand steadfast before God as witnesses for justice, even though it is against yourselves, your own parents or your own close relatives; whether it concerns a rich or a poor man, God stands closer to them both. Do not be led by any passion lest you deal unjustly. If you distort your testimony or decline to give it, God is still informed of what you do.

(The Qur'an, 4:135)

Any Abd (slave or man) authorized by Allah to ruler over certain people will never even have the smell of Paradise if he fails to look after them in an honest manner.

(Hadith of Bukhari)

When one of you is to supplicate, he should do so with full confidence and should not say, "Oh Allah, grant me if Thou will", for there is no power which can force the hand of Allah.

(Hadith of Bukhari)

The leader must be dependable. He should be accessible at all times, especially in emergencies. To demonstrate his dependability, he must be impartial, *exemplary* in conduct and act in full confidence.

EXEMPLARINESS

*Say, "Come I will recite what your
Lord has made binding on you.
Serve no other gods besides Him.
Show kindness towards both your
parents.
Do not kill your children because of
poverty; we shall provide for you as
well as for them.
Do not indulge in shameful acts, be
they open or secret.
Do not kill any person—for that God
has forbidden—except through (due
process of) law. He has instructed you
in this so that you may grow in
wisdom.*

Do not tamper with an orphan's wealth before he comes of age, except to improve it.

Give full measure and weight in all fairness. We do not charge any person with more than he can bear.

Whenever you speak, be just, even though it affects a close relative.

Fulfill God's covenant. Thus has He instructed you, so that you may take heed.

This is My Straight Road, so follow it and do not follow (other) paths which will separate you from Him. Thus has He instructed you so that you may do your duty.

(The Qur'an, 6:151-153)

There is nothing which weighs heavier in the balance than good character.

(Hadith of Ahmad)

May Allah have mercy on a person who is not difficult, but courteous when he sells, buys or asks for the payment of his dues.

(Hadith of Bukhari)

Whatever his other virtues, a leader must be exemplary, his behaviour must be exemplary, his attitude must be exemplary. But, as a general rule, he cannot be exemplary unless he is *fair*.

FAIRNESS

*We have sent our messengers
with explanations and sent
the scriptures and the scales
of justice down with them,
so that men may conduct
themselves with
fairness.*

(The Qur'an, 57:25)

*Love the one whom you love to a
certain degree (moderately) for perhaps
one day he will be someone for
whom you will feel hatred.*

Hate the one for whom you feel
hatred to a certain degree (moderately),
for perhaps one day he will be
the one whom you love.

(Hadith of Thirmidhi)

A leader must be fair in his dealings. He should be so impartial that nothing influences his decisions, except the facts. The leader must be justly balanced in his love and hate, and this should reflect in all his actions. This can be achieved if he is *genuine* in his approach.

GENUINENESS

Virtue does not reside in your turning your faces toward the east or west, but rather in believing in God (alone), the last Day, the Angels, the Book and the Prophets; and in the giving of one's wealth away, no matter how one loves it, to near relatives, orphans, the needy, the wayfarer and beggars and towards freeing captives; and in saying one's prayers and paying the alms levy. Those who keep their word whenever they promise anything, and are patient in suffering and hardship and in times of violence are the ones who are loyal and Godfearing.

(The Qur'an, 2:177)

All actions are judged by their intention.
There are two characteristics which are
not found together in a hypocrite:
"Good manners and an
understanding of religion."

(Hadith of Tirmidhi)

A person is perfect in his religion
(Islam) when he leaves alone that which
does not concern him.

(Hadith of Tirmidhi)

The leader must be genuinely interested in his task. His intentions should be clear and genuine and he must never be hypocritical. He should not take anything for granted. He must have a thorough understanding of each situation, so that an *honest* and loyal appraisal can be made, before embarking on any course of action.

HONESTY

You who believe, heed God and stand by those who are truthful.

(The Qur'an, 9:119)

Believe in Allah and be straight.

(Hadith Narrated by Abu Huraira)

There are three signs of the hypocrite: when he speaks, he lies.
when he makes a promises, he does not keep it. when he is trusted, he betrays.

(Hadith Narrated by Abu Huraira)

*It is falsehood enough when a person
narrates everything that he hears.*

(Hadith of Muslim)

Honesty is a virtue which we tend to take for
granted, but for a leader it is vital. He should be
absolutely honest to the point of never repeating
what he hears or reads, unless he verifies it. Dealing
with a problem and analysing it honestly will result
in a proper solution. This, of course, will require the
utmost *initiative.*

INITIATIVE

A good deed and an evil deed are not alike; repay (evil) with something that is finer and see how someone who is separated from you because of enmity will become a bosom friend.

(The Qur'an, 41:34)

A man passing along a road found a thorny branch lying across the road and pushed it away. Allah appreciated his action and forgave his sins.

(Hadith of Bukhari and Muslim)

*Every magnificent and important project
not begun with the praise of Allah,
remains defective.*

(Hadith of Abu Dawud)

Taking the initiative and following through are major requirements for a leader. He should not miss any opportunity of gaining ground, even if it is minor. One has to have a global plan of all requirements, so that one may initiate developments in stages with correct *judgement*.

JUDGEMENT

Whenever you judge between people, you should do so with fairness.

(The Qur'an, 4:58)

God is with the Judge, that is, His help and guidance are reaching him as long as he is just and fair; but when he departs (from the path of justice and fairness) and becomes unjust and tyrannical, the Lord leaves him alone and the Devil attaches himself to him.

(Hadith of Tirmidhi)

*A judge should not judge between two
persons when he is in an angry mood.*

(Hadith of Bukhari)

Correct judgement is essential for a good leader.
Being alert all the time will enhance his powers of
quick decision-making. This, however, is impossible
unless he has full *knowledge* of his responsibilities.

KNOWLEDGE

*The Month of Ramadan is when
the Qur'an was sent down as
a book of guidance for mankind
with explanations of right
and wrong.*

(The Qur'an, 2:185)

*Do not be quick to recite
the Qur'an before its revelation
has been accomplished, but
rather say: "Lord, increase
my knowledge."*

(The Qur'an, 20:114)

Do not acquire knowledge in order to compete with scholars or argue with the ignorant, or gain mastery over the gathering.

(Hadith of Ibn Majah)

When a person follows the path to the acquisition of knowledge, Allah will make it easy for him to enter Paradise.

(Hadith of Muslim)

Allah will not withdraw knowledge, snatching it away from people, but it will be withdrawn as a result of the death of learned persons. When no men of learning are available, people will appoint ignorant men as their leaders and will ask them for guidance on

religious matters, and they will give
fatwas (verdicts) without knowledge.
Thus they will go astray themselves and
will lead others astray.

(Hadith of Bukhari)

Knowledge is a basic requirement of management in general and of leadership in particular. Without knowledge, one cannot claim to be a leader. In addition to knowledge of his work, the leader should have a basic knowledge of the Qur'an and sunnah as applicable to his venture. The application of such knowledge in his daily routine will lead him to be very *liberal* in his approach.

LIBERALISM

And consult them in affairs (of moment)
then, when you have taken your decision,
put your trust in Allah, for Allah loves
those who put their trust in (Him).

(The Qur'an, 3:159)

When a ruler takes a decision after due
consideration and enquiry, and this decision
proves to be just and right, he is entitled to
be doubly recompensed. Should he, however,
after making full enquiries and taking proper
care, make a mistake, he will be entitled to a
lesser reward.

(Hadith of Bukhari)

Liberalism as opposed to dictatorship is a fine quality in a leader. He will consult with his colleagues and deputies to arrive at the most suitable solution to a particular problem. He should be freely approachable by those concerned and should have the *modesty* not to claim credit for his achievements.

MODEST

Be modest in the way you walk and lower your voice; the ugliest sound is a donkey's braying.

(The Qur'an, 31:19)

...God does not love the man who is arrogant and boastful.

(The Qur'an, 4:36)

Allah, the most exalted, has revealed to me that you should be courteous and cordial to each other, so that nobody may consider himself superior to another nor harm him.

(Hadith of Muslim)

*Modesty results in good alone
and nothing else.*

(Hadith of Bukhari and Muslim)

*Allah will not look at the person
who drags his garment (behind
him) out of his conceit.*

(Hadith of Bukhari)

Modest leaders are hard to find, as it extremely difficult to curb one's egoism. But the leader who is modest in order to make things easy for everyone is a truly unique person, whose modesty will be seen as a mark of *nobility*.

NOBILITY

Oh mankind, we have created you from a male and female and set you up as nations and tribes, so that you may recognise one another. The noblest among you before God are those of you who best perform their duty. God is all-knowing and wise.

(The Qur'an, 49:13)

The best among you are those who have the best manners.

(Hadith Narrated by Abdullah Ibn Amr)

*Virtue is good conduct, and sin is
that which pinches your mind
and makes you feel afraid that
people may come to know of it.*

(Hadith of Muslim)

*The most disgraceful title in the
estimation of Allah is the self-styled
King of Kings, or Emperor.*

(Hadith of Bukhari)

Nobility, which ranks high in the requirements for
leadership, is based on the possession of excellent
moral qualities. This has to be coupled with
organizing ability to reach the top.

ORGANIZATION

Recite your prayers at sunset,
at nightfall and
at down; the dawn
prayer has its witnesses.
Pray during the night as well;
an additional duty,
for the fulfilment of
which your lord may
exalt you to an
honourable station. Say,
"My Lord, let me enter
through a rightful
entrance and leave by a
rightful exit."

(The Qur'an, 17:78-80)

When you travel through fertile land, give the camels their share of the vegetation of the land, and when you travel through barren land, hasten your pace and thus conserve their energy. When you halt for the night, leave the track unoccupied, for it is also a passage for the beasts and a haunt of insects and reptiles during the night.

(Hadith of Muslim)

Prayer is not (valid) either when food has been served, or at a time when a person is in need of relieving himself.

(Hadith of Muslim)

A woman came to the Prophet, who ordered her to go away and come back again. She said, "What if I came and didn't find you?" Her tone implying that she might find him dead. The Prophet said, "If you should not find me, go to Abu Bakr."

(Hadith of Bukhari)

For a leader to be productive, he should be well organized and thoughtful, and should delegate authority to associates. These are major keys to success. Successful leaders are of sterling *personality.*

PERSONALITY

A lasting recompense awaits you (the Prophet) for yours is a sublime nature.

(The Qur'an, 68:4)

The servants of the Beneficent are those who walk upon the earth modestly, and when foolish ones address them, answer, 'Peace!'

(The Qur'an, 25:63)

The mainstay of leadership, a good personality, is essential to command the respect of followers. The leader should be very diplomatic in dealing with people so as to win their hearts. This will ensure a *quality* performance.

QUALITY

Indeed, he succeeds who purifies himself.
(The Qur'an, 87:14)

Beware of committing oppression, for on the Day of Resurrection, oppression will be darkness, and beware of Avarice, for avarice destroyed those who came before you; it led them into the shedding of blood and making lawful that which was forbidden for them.
(Hadith of Muslim)

Quality is the essence of leadership. All ventures will be judged by the quality of performance attained by the leader's purifying himself and not oppressing any of his followers in the maintenance of discipline. This cannot be achieved unless he takes *responsibility* for the outcome.

RESPONSIBILITY

God only holds a person responsible for whatever He has given him. God will grant ease following hardship.

(The Qur'an, 65:7)

Each one of you is a Guardian and responsible for those of whom he is in charge. The Ruler is a Guardian and thus responsible for his subjects.

A man is the Guardian of his family and is responsible for those under his care. In like manner, each one of you is a guardian and is responsible for what he is entrusted with.

(Hadith Related by Umar)

By any standard, the leader will be held responsible for his actions. Therefore, responsibility is important for proper management and true leadership. When you are responsible and act accordingly, you have to *sacrifice* much in order to fulfill your obligations.

SACRIFICE

*You will never attain to
virtue until you give in
alms what you dearly
cherish. God is aware of the
alms you give.*

(The Qur'an, 3:92)

*"What is the best Jihad?"
The Prophet was asked: "He
who strives against his own
self and his desires for the
cause of Allah," said the
Prophet.*

*Being wealthy does not
mean having a great amount
of property. True wealth is
self-contentment.*

(Hadith of Bukhari)

*One should never refuse
anything one is asked for.*

(Hadith of Bukhari)

No leader can deliver the goods unless he is prepared to sacrifice some of his leisure time in the interests of a top-quality performance. He should be content with what he possesses. This exemplary attitude will encourage *teamwork* among his associates.

TEAMWORK

*Cling one and all to the faith of
God, and do not be divided.
Remember the favours God bestowed
on you when you were enemies. He
united your hearts so that you
became brothers through His grace.*

(The Qur'an, 3:103)

*In a group of three persons, two
should not talk confidentially so as to
exclude the third.*

(Hadith of Bukhari)

Faithful believers are to each other as the bricks of a wall, supporting and reinforcing each other. So saying, the Prophet Muhammad clasped his hands by interlocking his fingers.

(Hadith of Bukhari)

You see the believers, as regards their being merciful among themselves, showing love among themselves and being kind among themselves, resembling one body, so that if any part of the body is not well, then the whole body shares the sleepiness and fever with it.

(Hadith of Bukhari).

The successful leader is one who can make others work for him with complete acceptance of his leadership. Nothing can be achieved without teamwork. For the members of a team to function to the best of their ability, they must be treated by their leaders with genuine kindness and understanding.

UNDERSTANDING

*This is a blessed Book We
have sent down, so follow it
and keep from evil, so that
you may receive mercy.*

(The Qur'an, 6:155)

*The Prophet used to talk
very clearly and distinctly
so that his audience would
understand the point he was
making.*

(Hadith of Abu Dawud)

Whenever the Prophet Muhammad is given the opportunity to choose between two affairs he always chooses the easier and more convenient. But if he is certain that it is sinful, he will stay as far away as he can from it. He has never avenged himself, but if the sanctity of Allah were violated, he would do so. That would be for Allah, not for himself. He is the last one to get angry and first to be satisfied. His hospitality and generosity are matchless. His gifts and endowments bespeak a man who does not fear poverty.

(Narrated by Hazrat 'Aishah hadith of Bukhari)

Understanding a problem and being able to explain it to the people around him are unique qualities in a leader. But he cannot be possessed of such understanding unless he is alert and has a keen sense of duty. The really good leader should be able to wear any 'hat' at any time, for, without being *versatile*, he will not be in a position to solve all problems.

VERSATILITY

O prophet, we have sent you forth as a witness, a bearer of good tidings and a warner; one who shall call people to God by His leave and guide them like a shining light. Proclaim to believers that they will have great bounty from God.

(The Qur'an, 33:45-47)

When you see a person seeking an object earnestly, assist him to attain his ends. And never ask for a reward except that given by Allah.

(Hadith of Ash-Shifa)

The ability to fill in any position at any time is a matchless quality in a good Commander-in-Chief. This attribute will make such an indelible impression on subordinates, that they will never feel indispensable, which is essential if the whole team is to work in unison, thereby reflecting the real leadership. The leaders' familiarity with all fields will convinces subordinates not only of his versatility but of his *wisdom*.

WISDOM

I swear by the declining day
that perdition shall be the lot
of man, except for those who
have faith and do good works,
who exhort each other to
justice and to fortitude.

(The Qur'an, 103:1-3)

A believer is not
stung twice from the
same hole.

(Hadith of Bukhari)

*There is to be no envy except
with regard to two kinds of
individuals: one to whom Allah
has given wealth, which he
strives to spend righteously, and
one to whom Allah has given the
wisdom of the Qur'an upon
which he models his behaviour
and which he teaches to others.*

(Hadith of Bukhari)

A wise leader, laudable in every respect, must also
be cheerful. As well as inspiring respect by virtue
of his honourable conduct, he must in a positive
way promote harmonious teamwork. At all times
he should feel *young* at heart.

YOUTH

The servants of God have nothing
to fear or regret.

(The Qur'an, 10:62)

"Indeed, from amongst the servants of Allah,
there are servants who are not prophets, whom
the prophets and martyrs will envy." The
Prophet was asked, "Who are they, so that we
may love them?" He replied, "They are the
people who love each other due to Allah's light,
not because of relationship or kinship. They do
not fear when the people fear, nor do they grieve
when the people grieve."

(Hadith of Tabari)

A youthful leader is a fearless leader. Feeling young is a very important factor of leadership, as it has a positive effect on one's behaviour. One should not only update one's knowledge *zealously* but also act fearlessly—of course, within the framework of Islam, so as to maintain the highest standards.

ZEAL

*No mortal knows what
bliss is in store for the
pious as a reward for
their labours.*

(The Qur'an, 32:17)

*Muhammad is the father of
no man among you, but (he
is) Allah's Messenger and
the Seal of the Prophet.
Allah is aware of everything.*

(The Qur'an, 33:40)

*When three people set out on
a journey, they should appoint
one of them as a leader.*

(Hadith of Abu Dawud)

The zeal which inspires a leader is made up of aggressive enthusiasm plus in-depth knowledge. It is an attribute which, for the sake of Allah, must be fostered. Without a zealous leader, no organization will prosper, so may Allah imbue you with proper zeal, so that you may become the ideal leader.

THE PROPHET AS LEADER

The qualities and manners of the Prophet Muhammad were unique. He was a man of very fine appearance and expression, he was thoroughly reliable and also zealous in the execution of his tasks. He was, moreover, extremely patient, merciful and generous. In courage, he was unparalleled, going through the most difficult times with the most admirable sangfroid. Far from being arrogant or proud, he was modest and, in his judgements, very accurate. Visiting the poor and the needy and entertaining them were some of his favourite occupations. He never felt superior, and used to attend himself to most of his personal requirements. Always fully in control of his temper, he was very fair in his treatment of others. Every situation was treated by him with sagacity and each was given his proper due so that the best result might be achieved. The Prophet's goals were righteousness and remembrance of the Almighty. His magnanimity, broad-mindedness and tolerance were all quite exceptional. He was cheerful, easy-going, pleasant and lenient. Above all, he was divinely guided.

ISLAMIC BOOKS

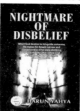

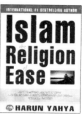

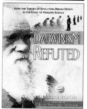

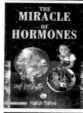

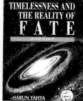

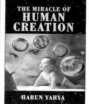

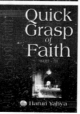

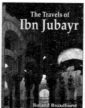

BOOKS FOR LEARNING ARABIC & ISLAMIC BOOKS

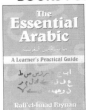
The Essential Arabic
A Learner's Practical Guide
Rafi'el-Imad Faynan

Let's Speak Arabic
Learn Arabic Conversation in just one week!
S.A. Rahman

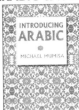
INTRODUCING ARABIC
MICHAEL MUMISA

Arabic Phrase Book

Teach Yourself ARABIC
A MODERN AND STEP BY STEP APPROACH
S.A. RAHMAN

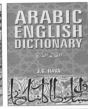
ARABIC ENGLISH DICTIONARY
J.G. HAVA

Islamic Medicine
EDWARD G. BROWNE

A BRIEF ILLUSTRATED GUIDE TO UNDERSTANDING ISLAM

Introducing Islam
A Simple Introduction to Islam
Maulana Wahiduddin Khan

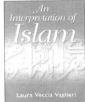
An Interpretation of Islam
Laura Veccia Vaglieri

THE ISLAMIC ART AND ARCHITECTURE
SIR THOMAS ARNOLD

Understanding Islam and the Muslims

A Dictionary of Muslim Names
PROF. S.A. RAHMAN

THE ESSENTIALS OF Islam

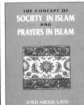
THE CONCEPT OF SOCIETY IN ISLAM AND PRAYERS IN ISLAM
SYED ABDUL LATIF

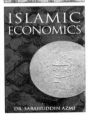
ISLAMIC ECONOMICS
DR. SABAHUDDIN AZMI

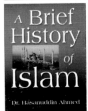
A Brief History of Islam
Dr. Hasanuddin Ahmed

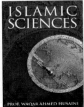
ISLAMIC SCIENCES
PROF. WAQAR AHMED HUSAINI

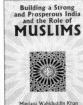
Building a Strong and Prosperous India and the Role of MUSLIMS
Maulana Wahiduddin Khan

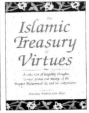
An Islamic Treasury of Virtues
A collection of inspiring thoughts, sayings, stories and maxims of the Prophet Muhammad ﷺ and his companions
Maulana Wahiduddin Khan

CHILDREN'S BOOKS

ISLAMIC BOOKS

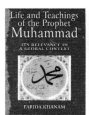
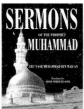

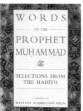

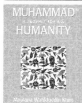
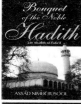
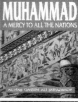

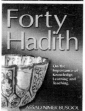
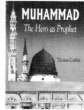
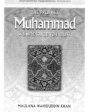

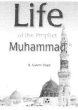

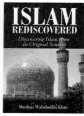

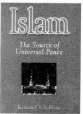